Graphing the Mystery

Book Three of
The Gift of Numbers
Math Fantasy Curriculum

Rachel Rogers and Joe Lineberry

Illustrations by ARTE RAVE

an imprint of
PROSPECTIVE PRESS LLC
1959 Peace Haven Rd, #246, Winston-Salem, NC 27106 U.S.A.
www.prospectivepress.com

Published in the United States of America by PROSPECTIVE PRESS LLC

GRAPHING THE MYSTERY

Text copyright © Rachel Rogers and Joe Lineberry, 2019
All rights reserved.
The authors' moral rights have been asserted.

Illustrations by ARTE RAVE
© Prospective Press, 2019
All rights reserved.
The illustrator's moral rights have been asserted.

ISBN 978-1-943419-48-7

Graphing the Mystery is the third volume in the Gift of Numbers math fantasy curriculum. For information on additional volumes in the series or for bulk sales, please send inquiries to education@prospectivepress.com

Printed in the United States of America
First paperback printing September, 2019

The text of this book is typeset in Mouse Memoirs
Accent text is typeset in Galindo

PUBLISHER'S NOTE

This book is a work of creative non-fiction with fictional fantasy elements. The people, names, characters, locations, activities, and events portrayed or implied by this book are the product of the author's imagination or are used fictitiously. Any resemblance to actual people, locations, and events is strictly coincidental. Multiple giraffes contributed to the development of this book.

Without limiting the rights as reserved in the above copyright, no part of this publication may be reproduced, stored in or introduced into any retrieval system, or transmitted–by any means, in any form, electronic, mechanical, photocopying, recording, or otherwise–without the prior written permission of the publisher. Not only is such reproduction illegal and punishable by law, but it also hurts the authors and illustrator who toiled hard on the creation of this work and the publisher who brought it to the world. In the spirit of fair play, and to honor the labor and creativity of the authors and illustrator, we ask that you purchase only authorized electronic and print editions of this work and refrain from participating in or encouraging piracy or electronic piracy of copyright-protected materials. Please give creators a break and don't steal this or any other work.

Dedicated to our amazing children:

Life was much better among the odd and even numbers. It was better because odd and even numbers were working together at More Children's Hospital. Using math operations, they were making more new numbers each day.

Life was also better because odd and even numbers were living together in fact families. What a nice change from the days when odd and even numbers didn't get along!

But there were still problems. Numbers were disappearing during the operations. No one knew when a number would vanish. One day after eating a healthy snack of peaches and cool mountain water, number 8 disappeared.

Thank goodness! Number 8 was living in a fact family with number 3 and number 11:

3 + ☐ = 11

So the family used the operation of subtraction to make a new number 8:

11 − 3 = 8

The kings wanted to stop the numbers from vanishing. Future boys and girls would run out of numbers, if they kept disappearing.

They decided to talk. They knew that fresh air and exercise would help them focus on a solution. They met outside on the hospital's walking trail.

The two kings turned a corner on the trail. They were surprised to see Detective 7 Science. He was in the bushes with his magnifying glass. They guessed he was looking for a clue to solve some mystery.

King More called out to Detective Science, "We have a mystery to solve. Can you help us? How do we find out what is causing our numbers to disappear?"

Detective Science joined their walk. He replied, "To solve this mystery, we need to look at all the information. We call that information "data." There may be clues in the data. What data do you have about the missing numbers?"

"The numbers began disappearing two months ago, when ghostly zero showed up," answered King Less. "Both even and odd numbers have disappeared. And we know that numbers vanished only during certain operations."

"You don't know for sure that zero is the cause. Maybe there is some cause that you haven't seen," said Detective Science.

"Do you know if more numbers are vanishing from just one operating room?" he continued. "Or do you know if more numbers disappear in the morning or afternoon?"

"Good questions," responded King More.

"I'll go ask Doctor Even to gather the data," said King Less.

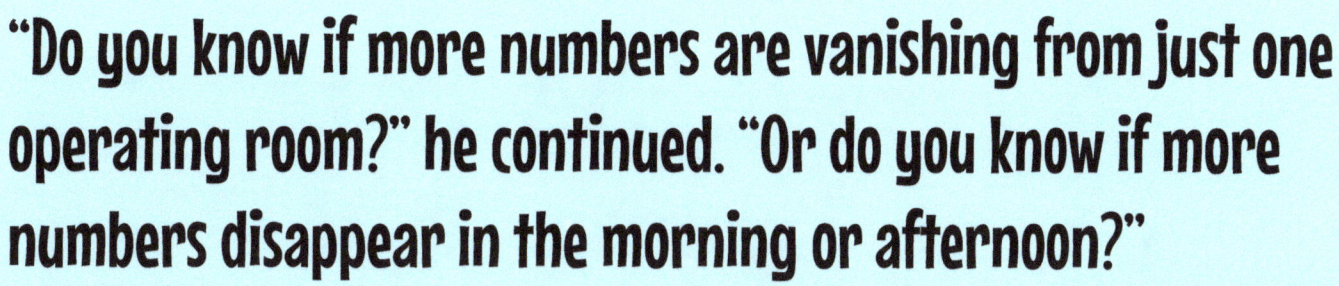

Doctor Even enjoyed working with data. He quickly found more information. He wanted to know where the numbers were when they vanished. He made a tally chart with the data.

Doctor Even decided to show the data in a graph. He thought a graph would make the information easier to understand. He needed some help with his graph, so he called his friend, Graph Giraffe.

Graph Giraffe was an extraordinary giraffe. She really liked graphs and computers, but she had a problem. Have you ever tried typing on a computer with giraffe hooves? It's not easy.

So her dad helped her out. He took her to see Dream Princess. The princess is an expert in making dreams come true. Dream Princess attached a special computer on the giraffe.

When Graph Giraffe arrived, she explained how her computer worked, "First, I collect data in a tally chart. I see you already have the tally chart. You are trying to find clues by comparing where numbers disappeared."

"Then I think about what type of graph I want to make with the data. Right now I'm thinking of a bar graph. Now look at my computer screen, and you will see the graph appear. It's like magic!"

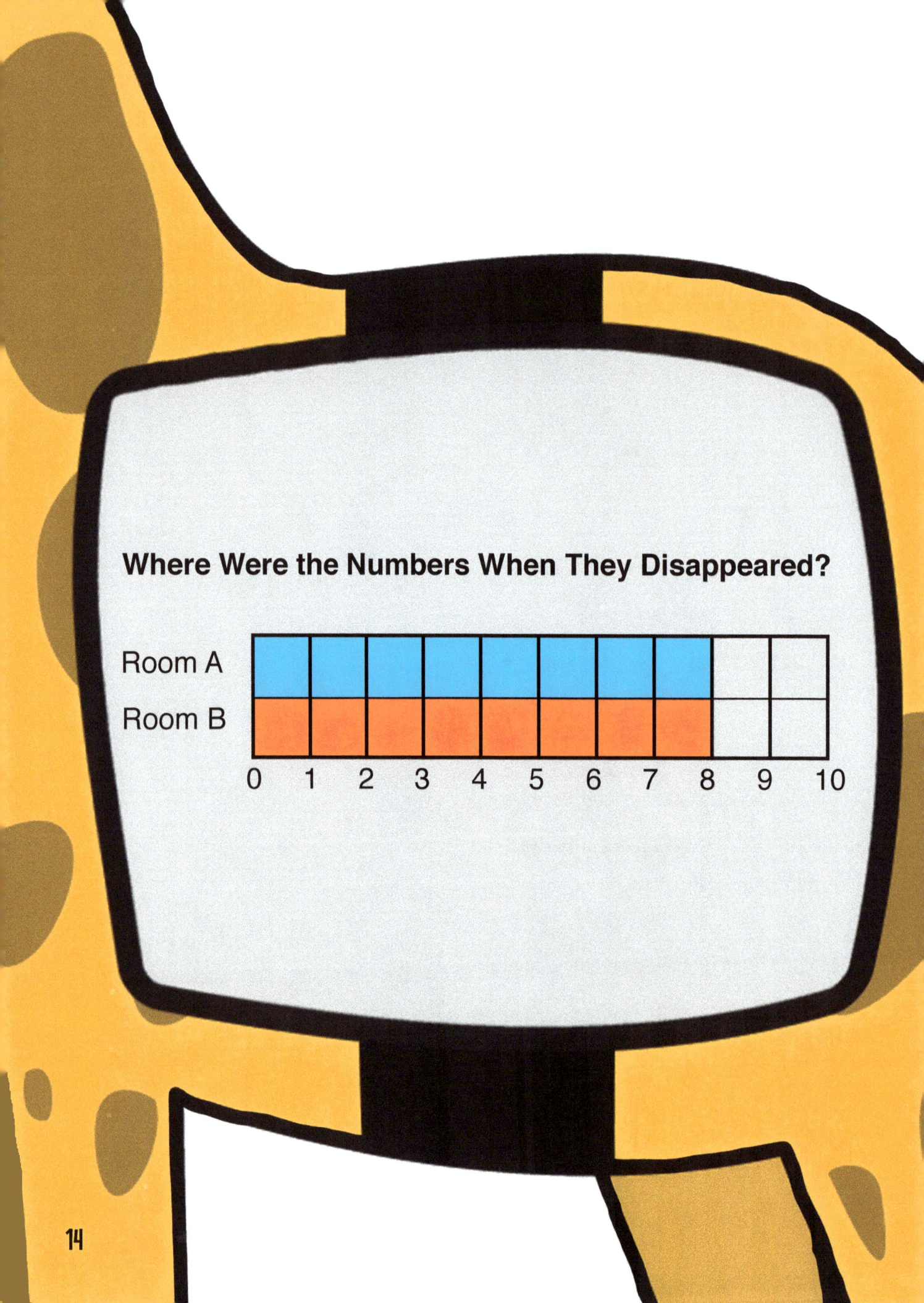

Sure enough, a bar graph appeared on the computer. Graph Giraffe looked down at the graph to see if it was correct. It had a title—

"Where Were the Numbers When They Disappeared?"

The two locations where numbers vanished were listed down the left side—

Operation Room A and Operation Room B.

There were little blocks for each location going across the graph.

- Eight blocks were colored blue for the eight numbers who vanished from Operation Room A.
- Eight blocks were colored orange for the eight numbers who disappeared from Operation Room B.

Graph Giraffe saw that her graph was complete and that it was correct. Then, guess what happened. The giraffe laughed. First, she snickered.

Then, she chuckled.

Finally, she cackled with laughter.

They all knew the graph was correct, because the giraffe only laughs when the graph is right.

Doctor Even was so excited. "Let's look for other clues in the data," he said. The group came up with two more tally charts of data:

Data, page 2
Numbers who disappeared before zero arrived:
Numbers who disappeared after zero arrived: 𝍫𝍫𝍫 𝍫𝍫 𝍫𝍫 |
Numbers who disappeared in morning operations: ||
Numbers who disappeared in afternoon operations: 𝍫𝍫 𝍫𝍫 ||||

Graph Giraffe thought about the data. This time she thought of pictographs instead of bar graphs. Two pictographs appeared on her computer screen.

When Did Numbers Start Disappearing?

Before Zero Arrived	
After Zero Arrived	

What Time of Day Did Numbers Disappear?

Morning Operations	
Afternoon Operations	

Key
Each ☺ = 2 Numbers Who Disappeared

Graph Giraffe laughed again. Doctor Even knew this was the signal that the graphs were correct.

But King Less was not so sure. He exclaimed, "Wait a minute! In the first pictograph, I only count eight smiley faces. I know that sixteen numbers vanished after zero arrived. Why did you laugh? There should be sixteen smiley faces."

Graph Giraffe stopped laughing and smiled. She understood the king's problem. She said, "Look at the key at the bottom of the graph, 'Each ☺ = 2 Numbers Who Disappeared.' Each smiley face stands for two missing numbers."

She pointed at the smiley faces and said, "Count the smiley faces by twos—2, 4, 6, 8, 10, 12, 14, 16."

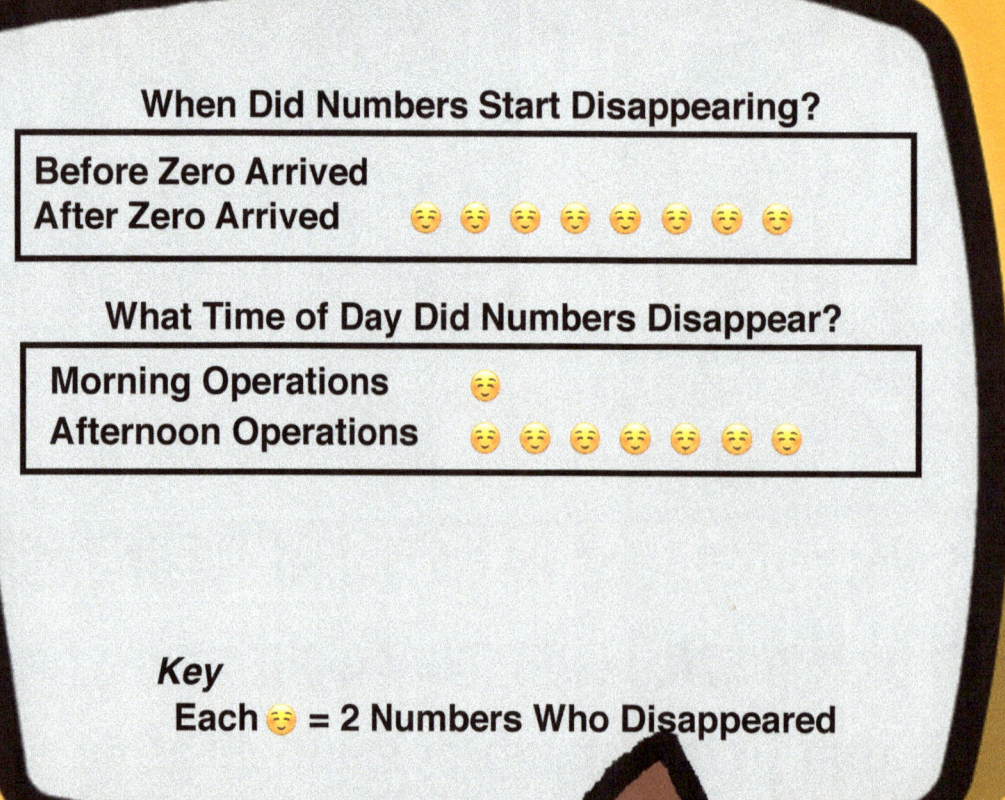

Graph Giraffe was right. She finished her laugh. Then she wiggled her nose, and all the graphs printed.

Doctor Even and King Less thanked Graph Giraffe for her help. They gathered the graphs and headed off to a meeting with Detective Science and King More.

Doctor Even was getting ready to present his graphs to the group. King More interrupted him. "Do you hear what I hear? Someone is laughing. What's going on?"

King Less winked at Doctor Even and said, "I think you're hearing things. Maybe it's just the wind."

(So who do you think was laughing?)

King More assumed it was the wind. He looked at Detective Science and asked, "What clues are we looking for in these graphs? How will they help us solve the mystery of the missing numbers?"

"We are looking for big differences in the data," said the detective.

"First, look at the graph of numbers who disappeared from each operation room—eight from each one. No difference there. We can guess that there is nothing in one of the operation rooms that is causing numbers to vanish."

When Did Numbers Start Disappearing?

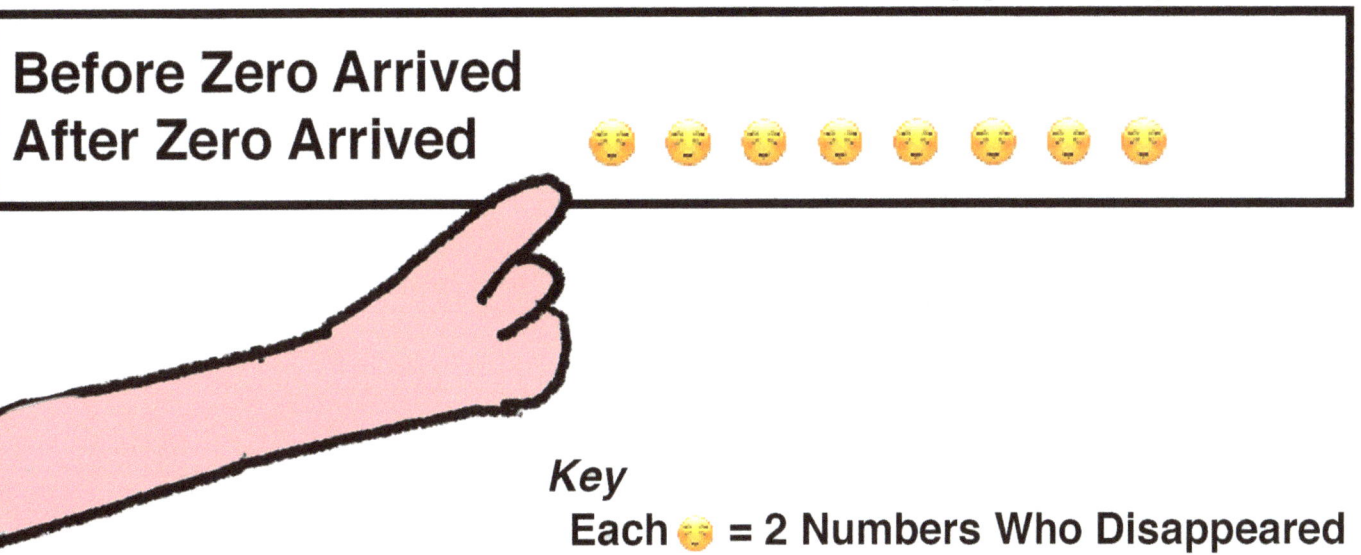

| Before Zero Arrived | |
| After Zero Arrived | 😢 😢 😢 😢 😢 😢 😢 😢 |

Key
Each 😢 = 2 Numbers Who Disappeared

Detective Science continued, "However, look at the big difference in the numbers who disappeared before and after zero arrived. That is a clue that zero may be causing the numbers to disappear."

"I knew it!" screamed King Less. "I have always thought it must be ghostly zero."

"Hold on," cried the detective. "We can't blame zero yet. He may not be causing the numbers to disappear."

"Look at the graph of numbers disappearing in the morning and in the afternoon," said Detective Science. "That's a big difference, too—two disappeared in the morning and 14 disappeared in the afternoon.

"There may be something else besides zero causing numbers to disappear. Whatever the cause, it has more effect in the afternoon."

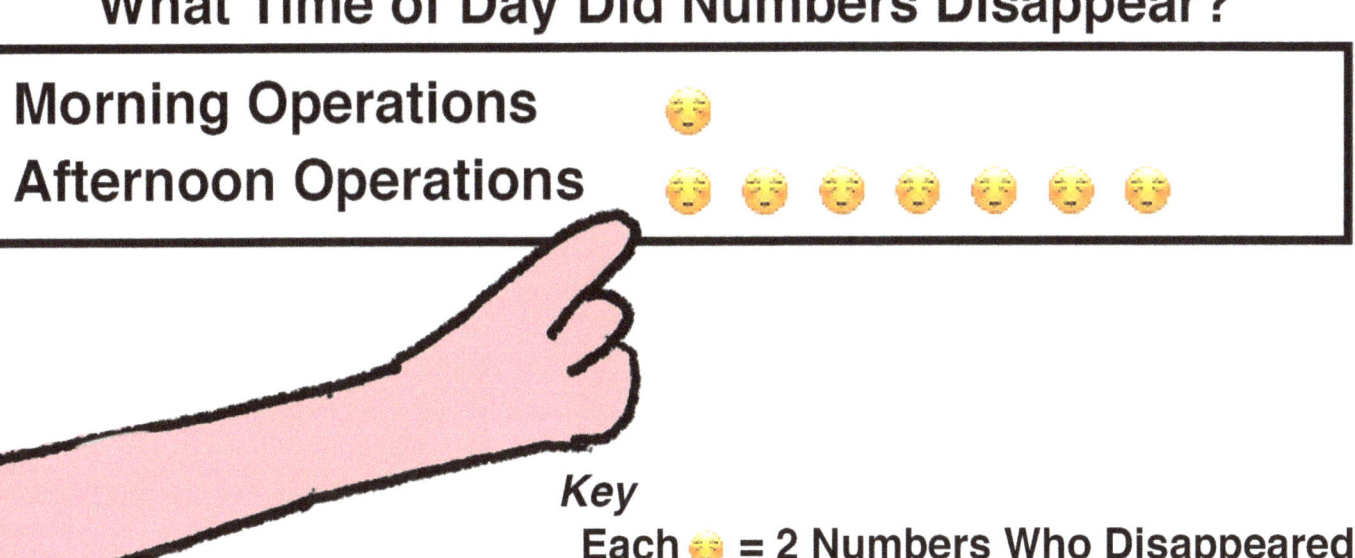

King More was frustrated. "Where do we go from here? Are we any closer to solving the mystery of the missing numbers? What do we do now?"

Doctor Even tried to calm everyone in the room. "Using these clues, we are guessing zero could be causing numbers to disappear. We are also guessing that something in the afternoon operations is the cause. We don't really know.

"Detective Science needs to develop a way to test our guesses. The detective and I have more work to do."

"You can do more work, if you want," King Less replied. "I'm going to find Dream Princess. She's smart. That's where Graph Giraffe got her computer. Maybe the Dream Princess has a magic formula that will stop our numbers from disappearing."

They all rushed out the door, hoping to solve the mystery of the missing numbers!

Graphing the Mystery Exercise

The numbers enjoyed eating healthy snacks. They voted for their favorite snacks by eating one of their favorite fruits. Using the data below—from votes of their choices of snacks—complete the bar graph.

Apple: 10   Banana: 7   Peach: 5   Orange: 3

Title: _____

Y-axis: Number of Fruit Choices (1–12)

Kinds of Fruit

Healthy Snacks Questions

1. Which was the most favorite snack?

2. Which was the least favorite snack?

3. How many types of fruit were eaten in all?

4. How many more apples were eaten than peaches?

5. If two more numbers chose bananas, how many votes would bananas have?

Discussion Questions

1. What is data?

2. How can you make data easier to understand?

3. King Less used data about missing numbers to try to solve why the numbers were disappearing. What did he find?

4. Do you think *Graphing the Mystery* is a good title for this book? Explain and give reasons to support your answer.

Exercise Solution

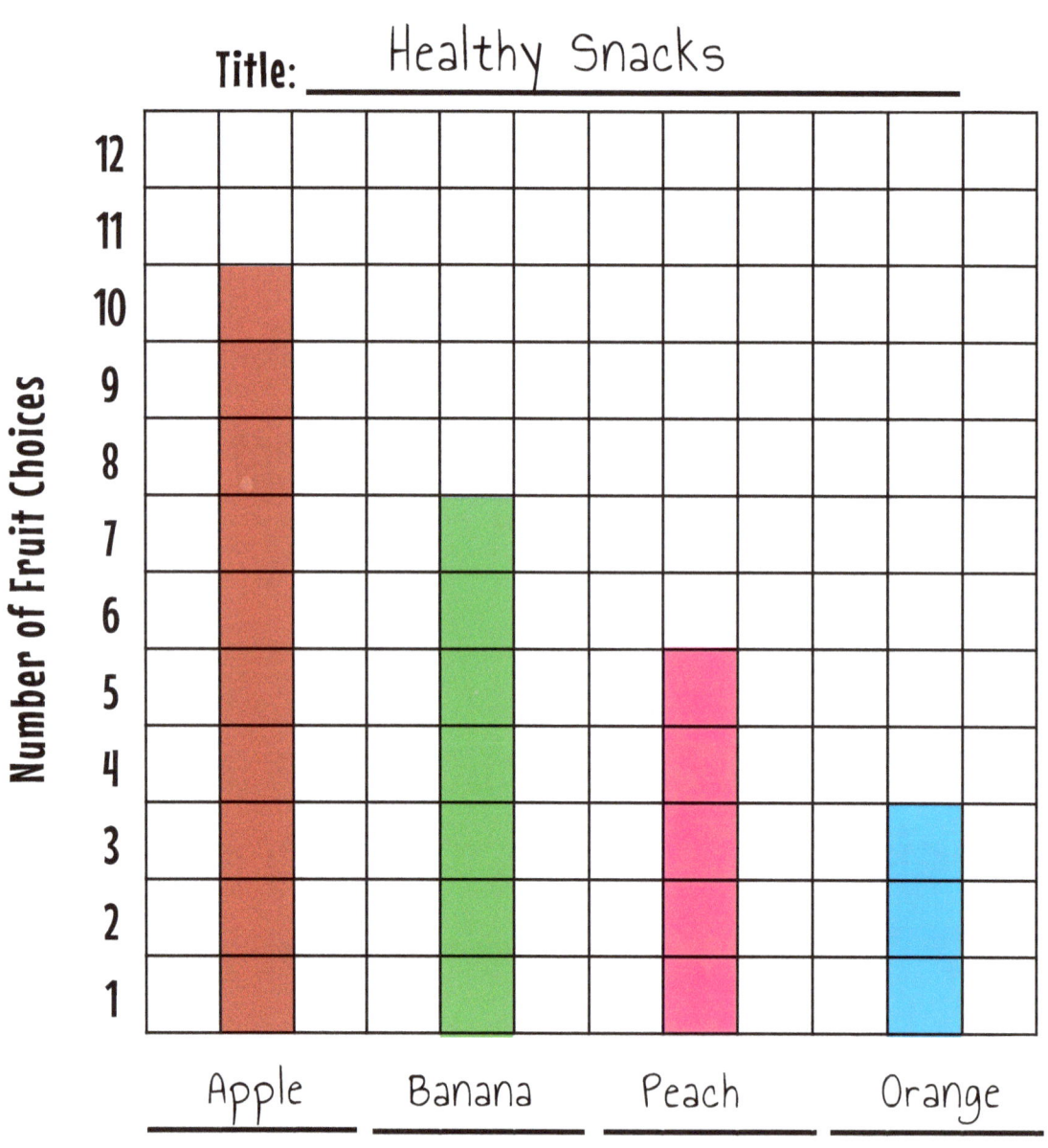

About the Authors

Rachel Rogers
is an elementary school teacher at Old Richmond Elementary School, Winston-Salem, NC. She has more than 35 years of experience teaching first, second, and third graders.

Joe Lineberry
told similar stories to his sons when they were growing up. He is also the author of *Let's Stop Playing Games: Finding Freedom in Authentic Living.*

About the Books

The Gift of Numbers
is a math fantasy curriculum that combines literature and mathmatics in a fun, age-appropriate series for second- and third-grade students.

- Volume 1: *Saved by Addition*
- Volume 2: *Surprised by Subtraction*
- Volume 3: *Graphing the Mystery*
- Volume 4: *Adventure with Fractions*
- Volume 5: *Multiplication Football*
- Volume 6: *The Experiment Game*
- Volume 7: *Division Gymnastics*

www.ingramcontent.com/pod-product-compliance
Lightning Source LLC
Chambersburg PA
CBHW051334110526
44591CB00026B/3000